Riba
In
Mubadalah

Nizar Abdulrahman Alshubaily

2021

Table of Contents

Also By The Author

Riba Revisited Series:

Riba In Jewelry

Riba Complexity

Riba In Contracts

Riba: The Book Of Quotes

The Names Of Riba

A Sale Is Like Riba

The Hadith Of Riba

Myths Of Riba

The Verses Of Riba

Essays In Islamic Finance Series:

Essays In Islamic Finance I

Essays In Islamic Finance II

Essays In Islamic Finance III

Riba In Mubadalah

Nizar Abdulrahman Alshubaily

A Summary of Scholarly Views on Riba in Changing Money into Smaller Denominations

Volume I

Riba Revisited Series

2021

Riba In Mubadalah

Volume I

Riba Revisited Series

Cover Page: Photo of Manuscript of "Sahih Al-Bukhari" courtesy of Alukah.net

EBOOK ISBN: 9781393310846

In

Memory

Of

My

Parents

Preface

have been involved in the Islamic Finance industry since the 1980s. I have seen
ts slow beginnings and its subsequest rapid rise. I can speak with confidence, that
he subject of Riba is the most confusing for most observers, students, and even
professionals in the industry.

This book is a lengthened version of a series of articles I wrote entitled "Riba in
Mubadalah", and is part of a series of articles on Riba entitled "Riba Revisited".

started the series in September 2019, and it already includes forty articles on
he subject of Riba.

My hope was and is, to help people navigate such a difficult subject; a subject
very misunderstood and has the most important bearing on the subject of the
tructuring of Islamic Finance products.

Whilst there are many books on Riba in Arabic, I noticed that in English there
were very few. In addition, the ones available rarely treated subjects such as
his one. They usually stay close to the main headings without adventuring into
unusual areas of investigation.

t is also a subject that takes place in our everyday lives, often without us noticing
he difference between the forbidden and permissible.

Nizar Abdulrahman Alshubaily,

January 2021

Introduction

RIBA is a most mysterious subject. Even to our great predecessors it proved to be a very enigmatic prospect. Where does Riba manifest itself? How? Where does one draw the line? How does one know whether a transaction is Riba, or just looks like it?

Sometimes it is clear, and other times it is like being in a hall of mirrors. One wonders whether it is a true reflection, or just an illusion.

It is an action that practically every human has done in his lifetime. Changing money. Not the changing into another currency, but getting change for larger bills.

What rules govern this type of transaction? What are the pitfalls of which to be careful? What are the views and disputes of scholars?

In this brief book, I investigate this issue and hopefully shed light on some of the issues and point out the areas of danger and dispute.

This book requires a certain amount of knowledge of the subject of Riba and 'Fiqh Al-Mu'amalat'. Whilst the book is not difficult by any measure, it still does require a certain amount of understanding of issues, without which, the concepts may seem vague.

The book however, has been written in very easy language. It should feel as if I were speaking to you, the reader, face to face. I have done my best to remove any hint of academic pretensions in order to facilitate the ease of reading, and the learning experience.

Many books sometimes forget that the reader learns best by seeing an example from daily life, against which he can compare a particular Shari'ah issue. This is too often missing in many books on Islamic Finance.

Riba is a subject that no book on Islamic Finance should go without. Riba is such an important subject, and is often a very divisive one as well. Many think they understand it well, only to find they are confounded when asked questions.

Riba is the most fascinating subject in Islamic Finance. The prohibition of Riba is essentially the main driver in creating products compliant with Shari'ah.

Other prohibitions, whilst important, can be found often in existing conventional regulations. Thus, it is Riba, which is the primary cause of concern in the design of Islamic Financial Products.

This is a very important topic due to the similarities between Riba and some aspects of certain transactions. Effectively, the less you know, the more likely you are to confuse an aspect with Riba.

Riba can be so difficult to fully comprehend that even great scholars in the past admitted their difficulties with it, and even made some rash judgments. Great men have tried to unveil its mystery, and many have failed.

Al-Ghazzali (Died Hijri 505): "The issue of Riba... is one of the most mysterious issues."

Ibn Kathir (Died Hijri 774): "Riba is one of the most confusing issues for scholars."

Al-Shatibi (Died Hijri 790): "Riba is a subject with a concealed face for the diligent, and is one of the most hidden issues whose meaning is unknown till today."

Even greater men, and earlier than the above, struggled with it.

Umar ibn Al-Khattab (RAA): "I am afraid we might have exaggerated in Riba ten times for fear of it", and "We have left out nine tenths of Halal from fear of Riba."

Riba Al-Buyu'
Summary Of The Riba Of Sales

"Gold for gold, silver for silver, wheat for wheat, barley for barley, dates for dates, and salt for salt, like for like and equal for equal, hand to hand. If these classes differ, then sell as you wish if it is hand to hand."

The Prophet

"Sahih Muslim"

THE Riba of Sales (Al-Buyu') has always confused some, but spending some time on it, helps clarify many issues.

There are two categories: 1) Foods, and 2) Metals.

The metals such as gold and silver were generally used as money.

The Foods were popular staples of the time.

The rules are that if you are trading items within the same category, there can be no delay at all.

The items, if from the same category, whether it is gold against gold, silver against silver, gold against silver, dates against barley, wheat against salt, must always be exchanged immediately, during the Majlis (session of contract). If any delay is present, then this is Riba Al-Nasaa' (also called by some Nasee'a).

The only difference is that if the items, within the same category are also the same genus such as gold against gold, silver against silver, dates against dates, wheat against wheat, then they need to be exchanged in equal weights (for gold and silver), or equal volumes (for the foods). Any inequality triggers Riba Al-Fadl.

If however, there is a trade between items from different categories, such as dates from The Foods category, and gold, from The Metals category, then deferment and inequality are both permitted.

I have used a simple chart, used by many, that shows the permitted and forbidden exchanges, hopefully making it easier to understand for those unfamiliar with the rules.

An important point to remember: when we state "Immediate Exchange", we mean by both parties. When immediate exchange (Taqabud) is not demanded, this does not mean that both counterparts can be delayed; it means that only one of the items could be delayed.

	Gold	Silver	Wheat	Barley	Dates	Salt
Gold	■					
Silver		■				
Wheat			■			
Barley				■		
Dates					■	
Salt						■

■ Equality (Tamathul) and Immediate Exchange (Taqabud) Demanded

▨ Only Immediate Exchange (Taqabud) is Demanded

□ Free: Neither Equality, Nor Immediate Exchange is Demanded

The chart shows the rules for the exchange of the named Ribawi items against each other.

Black is when an item is being exchanged with the same item, meaning itself, being of the same genus, such as gold against gold. In this case, the rules forbid any inequality in the weights or volumes exchanged (Riba Al-Fadl), and they also forbid any delay in the possession of the items by the contracting parties beyond the session of contract (Majlis), (Riba Al-Nasaa').

The grey is between different items, meaning a different genus such as gold against silver, or wheat against dates, but of the same category. In this case, quality of volumes or weights is not demanded, and there is no Riba Al-Fadl. However, they must still be exchanged immediately within the session of contract, as such, in this yellow area, Riba would only exist in deferment (Nasee'a).

The white area means there is no Riba, either Al-Fadl or Al-Nasaa', since the items being exchanged are of completely different categories, meaning Foods against Metals.

The 2 parts of Riba Al-Buyu' are:

1. Riba Al-Fadl: Inequality where Equality is Demanded.
2. Riba Al-Nasaa': Delay where Immediate Exchange is Demanded.

The Golden Rule: "Ignorance of Equality is Knowledge of Inequality", this means that any lack of knowledge of equality in an exchange where equality is demanded, is automatically Riba.

For Gold and Silver, the exchange between these genera is By Weight as was the custom of the people of Makkah during the period of The Revelations, while for the four Foods, the exchange is by volume as was the custom of the people of Madinah during the period of The Revelations.

Other items may be included, such as paper money to the Metals/Currency category, and this would be by custom, so paper money is exchanged by the same value, and not by the weight of the paper. Paper money of course is used the same as gold and silver, meaning it has the same "Illah", which is called "Thamaniyyah", denoting that paper money, like gold and silver is used as a price to pay for items, and thus carries the same rules.

Differences in Value or Quality are Immaterial to the exchanges (except in paper money), so for example, low quality dates versus higher quality dates, the exchange must still be equal in volume.

Gold and Silver also includes Jewelry. This for some is disputed, as some scholars both classical and modern, regard jewelry as having moved from being a price as in a gold coin, to become a good, like clothes, and thus can be traded on a deferred basis. But the current consensus treats jewelry the same as a gold coin and it must be exchanged against other gold items by weight.

Scholars disputed whether other types of foods also apply, based on their characteristics, but there is generally agreement that gold and silver would also include any items used as money, such as paper money.

Chapter One
Mubadalah And Sarf

"Riba is of two kinds, Clear (Jaliyy), and Invisible (Khafiyy).

The Clear Riba was forbidden because of its great harm, and the Invisible Riba was forbidden because it is a means to the Clear Riba.

The prohibition of the first is as a Purpose, and the prohibition of the second is as a Means."

Ibn Al-Qayyim

"A'alam Al-Muwaqi'in"

WHAT about paying 50 Dirhams for an object that is 40 Dirhams and receiving the object, but your change, the 10 Dirhams, is delayed?

What if you ask for change, and were told to return later for your change as the storeowner doesn't have any at the time; or you receive some of the change and are asked to return another day for the rest? Or you receive some of the change, and are asked to take an item instead of the change you are owed?

What are the rules? What are the different views?

There is a reason why the Hanbali School attached the Book of Sarf with the Book of Riba, as we shall see.

Some call getting change as Mubadalah since it is simply an exchange of items in the same currency, others call all exchanges as Mubadalah, while others call it Sarf, or Musarafah, or even Muratalah if it is between two currencies or items of money of the same kind, usually of the metallic type such as gold and silver by weights.

Sarf, for some is the exchange of two currencies even if they are of the same kind while for others, it is usually given as a name if the two items are of a different kind such as two different currencies or gold against silver, whereas Muratalah is when the two items are the same, such as gold against gold or silver against silver being exchanged by weight.

This is how The Maliki School has defined it:

> **"Sarf is selling Naqd (money) against a different kind, while Muratalah is selling Naqd (money) against its own kind." (1)**

And here is another reference and explanation of the above, to clarify the point The Malikis have a somewhat different terminology when it comes to the word Mubadalah:

> **"The Malikis describe Sarf as the sale of currency against a different kind, such as gold against silver. As for selling currency against its own kind, such as gold against gold, or silver against silver, they called it by a different name, and said: if the types are the same, and the sale is by weight, then it is Muratalah, and if it is by number, then it is Mubadalah (when the exchange is in numbers, meaning a currency is exchanged into a different number components.)" (2)**

And it was also mentioned in "Al-Sharh Al-Sagheer" by Al-Dardeer (Died Hijri 1201):

> **"And Mubadalah is permitted in gold and silver, and it is selling the currency, whether gold or silver against its own kind, meaning gold for gold or silver for silver by numbers, such as ten Dinars for ten Dinars, hand to hand..." (3)**

In the same book above, is also included in the margins, an explanation of Al-Dardeer's work, by Ahmad bin Muhammad Al-Sawi (Died Hijri 1241):

"His saying: "And Mubadalah is permitted" means therefore that selling a currency against a different currency is called a Sarf, and against the same currency, is either a Muratalah, which is the sale of currency against its own kind by weight...or a Mubadalah as has been identified by the writer (Al-Dardeer), and as stated by Ibn Arafah (Died Hijri 803), the sale of an item against its own kind by numbers, and so his saying 'against the same', excludes Sarf, and his saying 'by numbers', excludes Muratalah." (3)

For other schools, Sarf includes both, currency against another currency, and against its own kind, this one is from the Hanbali School:

"It is a sale of money against money, the same or different...and immediate possession in the Majlis (session of contract) is a condition of its validity, stated by Ibn Al-Munther as a consensus..." (4)

From the Hanafi School:

"Sarf is a name of a type of sale, which is the exchange (Mubadalah) of money against money..." (5)

And from the Shaefe'i School:

"The Sale of money against the same type and other types is called Sarf..." (6)

The famous dictionary Al-Mu'jam Al-Waseet calls such a sale as Sarf if the currencies are different, however they define this as the meaning within Economics:

"The exchange (Mubadalah) of a national currency against a foreign currency." (7)

Dr. Ahmad Al-Baz explains the reason for the views of the Maliki School:

"It appears that the Malikis use the linguistic meaning of Sarf. As we have mentioned, Sarf in the language of the Arabs had perhaps a meaning of changing something into another, and gold against gold, or silver against silver, do not have that change into something else.

But when gold is sold against silver, then change has taken place, since the seller has changed what he has in gold into silver, or the reverse, as well as the buyer. This is what the linguistic meaning demands. Thus, the Maliki definition that Sarf is the sale of a currency against a different kind is well founded from the linguistic side." (8)

Sheikh Bin Uthaimeen gives a different linguistic interpretation of the word Sarf:

"...Sarf in language is the sound...and Sarf is the sale of money against money, you sell for example gold against silver, or silver against silver, that is Dirhams against Dirhams, or Dirhams against Dinars, and it was called Sarf because they used to weigh the Dirhams and Dinars, they used to sell by weight, when we put them in scales, they have a "Sareef", meaning sound, that is why it is called Sarf." (9)

There's no dispute that if the transaction is a currency sale, or Sarf, that the exchange between the two amounts must be immediate, there is consensus on this issue.

This can be seen in many Fiqh books as well as summary books of particular schools such as Majallat Al-Ahkam Al-Shar'iyyah of the Hanbali School:

"It is a condition of Sarf that there is immediate exchange (Taqabud) in the Majlis (session of contract), if the parties separate before that, it is voided..." and "It is permissible to separate the transaction in Sarf, if possession takes place in some (of the amount), but the parties separate before possession of the rest, then in what was possessed it is correct and voided in the rest." (10)

In the Hanafi school we can read this also:

"Sarf is a sale if both counterparts are prices, thus if one sells gold for gold or silver for silver, it is not permitted except in equality regardless of the quality or fabrication, and immediate exchange must take place before separation (of the parties), and if one sells gold for silver, inequality is permitted, but immediate exchange is demanded and any delay is forbidden, and if they separate in Sarf before exchanging the counterparts or one of them, the contract is voided." (11)

This is also mentioned in "Al-Mughni":

"Everything where inequality has been forbidden, so has delay also been forbidden, without any known dispute, and separation (between parties) before possession is forbidden..." (12)

And one last mention by Ibn Rushd, the grandson (Died Hijri 595):

"The conditions of sarf:

The jurists agreed that among the conditions of sarf is that it should be immediate (najiz), however, they disagreed about the time in which this meaning is realized. Abu Hanifa and al-Shafi'i said that sarf is immediate if it takes place before the two parties to sarf separate, irrespective of possession being prompt or delayed. Malik said that if possession is delayed within the session, sarf is void, even if they have not parted, so much so that he disapproved the fixing of a time in it." (13)

As for consensus (Ijmaa'), this has been reported by Ibn Al-Munther (Died Hijri 318):

"There is consensus from everyone from whom I have memorized, that the two parties in Sarf, if they separate before possession, then the Sarf is corrupted." (14)

Of course the basis for this consensus is the Hadith by Ubada bin Al-Samit:

"Gold for gold, silver for silver, wheat for wheat, barley for barley, dates for dates, and salt for salt, like for like and equal for equal, hand to hand. If these classes differ, then sell as you wish if it is hand to hand." (15)

Ibn Al-Qayyim states:

"It was forbidden to separate in Sarf, and the sale of a Ribawi against its kind, before possession, so that it is not taken as an excuse to Delay, which is the fundamental aspect of Riba. They were protected from its proximity, by demanding immediate possession." (16)

As we have stated earlier, there is no dispute that if the contract is in fact Sarf, then it is forbidden to separate before mutual exchange. The issue here: I changing money into smaller pieces part of a contract of Sarf or is it a different contract where the rules of Sarf do not apply.

After all, a Sarf conract as we shall see, has its intention a profitable exchange, whereas Mubadalah, (or any other name chosen), where money is changed into smaller pieces, has as its intention benevolence.

References

1) Al-Dusuqi, "Hashiat Al-Dusuqi Ala Al-Sharh Al-Kabeer", (Cairo: Dar Ihya' Al-Kutub Al-Arabiyyah), Volume 3, p.2.

2) "Al-Mawsu'a Al-Fiqhiyyah Al-Kuwaitiyyah", (Kuwait: Dar Al-Safwa Publishers, 1992), Volume 26, "Sarf", p. 348.

3) Al-Dardeer, "Al-Sharh Al-Sagheer", (Cairo: Dar Al-Ma'aref, 1986), Volume 3, p. 63.

4) Al-Bahuti, "Kashaf Al-Qinaa'", (Riyadh: Dar Alam Al-Kutub, 2003), Fasl fi Al-Musarafah, Volume 5, p. 1495.

5) Al-Sarakhsi, "Al-Mabsut", (Beirut: Dar El-Marefa, 1989), Volume 14, p. 2.

6) Al-Sharbini, "Mughni Al-Muhtaj", (Beirut: Dar El-Marefa, 1997), Volume 2, p. 34.

7) Al-Mu'jam Al-Waseet, (Cairo: Maktabat Al-Shurooq Al-Dawliyyah, 2004), p. 513.

8) Dr. Abbas Ahmad Al-Baz, "Ahkam Sarf Al-Nuqud wa Al-Umlat", (Amman: Dar Al-Nafa'es, 1999), p. 26.

9) Sheikh Muhammad bin Salih Al-Uthaimeen, "Al-Sharh Al-Mumti'", Al-Dammam: Dar Ibn Al-Jawzi, 2002), Volume 8, Bab Al-Riba wa Al-Sarf, p. 449.

10) Majallat Al-Ahkam Al-Shar'iyyah, (Jeddah: Tihama Publications, 1981), Clauses 474-475, p. 191.

11) Al-Qadduri, "Mukhtasar Al-Qadduri", (Beirut: Dar Al-Kotob Al-Ilmyah, 1997), Bab Al-Sarf, p. 90.

12) Ibn Qudamah, "Al-Mughni", (Riyadh: Dar Alam Al-Kutub, 1997), Volume 5, p. 61.

(13) Ibn Rushd, "The Distinguished Jurist's Primer", (Reading: Garnet Publishing, 1994), translated by Professor Imran Nyazee, Volume II, The Book of Sarf, p. 235.

(14) Ibn Al-Munther, "Al-Ishraf", (Ras Al-Khaimah: Maktabat Makkah Al-Thaqafiah, 2005), Volume 6, p. 61.

(15) Sahih Muslim, (Beirut: Al-Maktaba Al-Asriyyah, 2002), Kitab Al-Musaqa wa Al-Muzara'a, Bab Al-Sarf, No. 4063 (1587), p. 598.

(16) Ibn Al-Qayyim, "A'alam Al-Muwaqq'in", (Al-Dammam: Dar Ibn Al-Jawzi, 2002), Volume 5, pp. 57-58.

Chapter Two
"Fakk Al-Nuqud

"Riba is a subject with a concealed face for the diligent, and is one of the most hidden issues whose meaning is unknown till today."

Al-Shatibi

"Al-Muwafaqat"

WE have called the contract of changing money into smaller pieces as Mubadalah before. But there is another name more apt for such a contract, and that is "Fakk Al-Nuqud".

Al-Nuqud of course is the plural of Naqd, which is basically money, originally gold and silver coinage, but lately it includes paper cash. The word "Fakk" means to exchange for something smaller, originally meant to take something apart, and thus the term "Fakk Al-Nuqud" is defined in the dictionaries as:

"The exchange of a large piece for smaller pieces." (1)

Dr. Muhammad Al-Mohaimeed, Professor of Fiqh, Qassim University in Saudi Arabia, who provided the above explanations in his paper, also makes the following observations on the terminology, where he defines the name of "Fakk Al-Nuqud" as "Aqd Al-Fakkah" or contract of change:

"The difference between the contract of Fakkah and Mubadalah is...every Fakkah is Mubadalah but not every Mubadalah is Fakkah, when it is an exchange (Mubadalah) of a large piece of currency into smaller pieces, it is called Fakkah, while an exchange

with something else is not Fakkah...Every buying and selling is Mubadalah, but not every Mubadalah is buying and selling...

The difference between the Contract of Fakkah and the contracts of Bai' (sale) and Sarf (currency exchange), is like the difference with a Qard, they agree in the picture but not the intention, the contract of Fakkah, just as a Qard has as its purpose, Benevolence and help, while the contracts of Bai' and Sarf are for profit." (2)

This is called "Fakkah" by other people as well such as Dr. Yusuf Al-Shubaily:

"...This is the issue of "Fakkah" as known in common language, for example a person has 100 Riyals and wants change, so he goes into a store and asks the seller for change, or buys something from the store, something simple such as a pop drink or sweets, or others, and what remains for example is 90 Saudi Riyals..." (3)

Sheikh Khaled Al-Mosleh also calls it the contract of "Fakkah' when asked a question regarding changing money:

"The closer opinion is that it is not compulsory to achieve simultaneity and not delaying in this issue, and it is permissible to delay, Regardless of whether we view paper money as equivalent to gold and silver, as the majority state, or it takes the rulings of "Fuloos" as others state.

This does not prevent delay in the contract of "Fakkah", since this contract in all its aspects, when currencies are the same, is a contract of benevolence and goodness, and not a contract of Mu'awadah (for profit compensatory exchange)." (4)

It is also the case that this is called "Fakkah" in Sudan, and was called this name by The Islamic Fiqh Academy of Sudan when they ruled that exchanging an amount of money or currency with the same kind, meaning when someone wants change, must be with equality (Tamathul) and no difference is allowed:

"The Islamic Fiqh Academy in Khartoum has released a fatwa that prohibits the sale of the same kind of money and currency (Al-Fakkah) by different prices, and has stated that this is of the forbidden Riba in Shari'ah." (5)

Islamweb.net, a popular website that provides online questions and answers on Islamic issues has also provided a fatwa on this issue, and they call such an action as "Fakkah":

"It is not permissible to sell paper currency for a lesser amount of metal currency or other, as it is the same kind, and what is called "Fakkah", or "Tasreef", is in reality a sale, and at the time of Mubadalah (Exchange) when the currency is the same, are two conditions..." (6)

Perhaps we can just make it easier for definition, to list the names and their meanings:

Muqayadah: Exchange between two commodities (not prices).

Sarf: Exchange between two different currencies (for others, it's still called Sarf even if they are the same currency).

Muratalah: Exchange between the same currencies, by weight (gold for gold).

Mubadalah: Exchange based on numbers, a higher denomination note for several smaller notes.

Fakk Al-Nuqud: Same as Mubadalah above, but a newly named contract.

So whether you wish to call changing money Mubadalah or "Fakk Al-Nuqud", that is not the issue, however, where there is an issue, as will be seen later, is whether it is a contract of Sarf and its rules apply.

This is an extremely important factor in determining its regulations, as Dr. Al-Mohaimeed has stated: "the contract of Fakkah just as a Qard has as its purpose Benevolence and help, while the contracts of Bai' and Sarf are for profit."

In fact, in the Arab world, we call it getting change as "Fakkah"; we actually ask the shop manager or bank teller if he has "Fakkah" for a 100 Dirham bill for example. Or if we do not have change for an item, we say: we don't have any "Fakkah".

In this book, we shall use the classical name for such a contract and call it "Mubadalah".

There are numerous varieties of this situation and we will try to seek the best answers for each, based on the intention:

I.   If the intention is receiving change, and the change is delayed fully
II. If the intention is receiving change, and the change is delayed partially
III. If the intention is a Sale, and the change is delayed
IV. If the intention is receiving change and an item is purchased, without declaration to the seller, and the change is delayed
V.   If the intention is receiving change, and it is declared to the seller, and an item is included against the remaining change
VI. If the intention is to receive change but where there is inequality between the amounts due to a fee or a benefit
VII. The unequal exchange between paper money and metal money (coins), is this permissible?

References

1) Al-Mu'jam Al-Waseet, (Cairo: Maktabat Al-Shurooq Al-Dawliyyah, 2004), p. 698.

2) Dr. Muhammad Al-Mohaimeed, "Ahkam Fakk Al-Nuqud", 2012, pp. 12-13.

http://almohaimeed.net/up/book/alnqod.pdf

3) Dr. Yusuf Al-Shubaily, "Fiqh Al-Mu'amalat Al-Masrafiyyah", 2006, (written from audiotapes by www.shamela.ws), p. 67.

4) Sheikh Khalid bin Abdullah Al-Mosleh, January 2, 2014. https://almosleh.com/ar/16946

5) The Islamic Fiqh Academy, Khartoum, Sudan, Printed in Alrakoba newspaper, 20 May 2012.

https://www.alrakoba.net/570661/

6) Islamweb.net, The Ruling on "Fakk Al-Nuqud" for a percentage, Fatwa 183329, 12 July 2012.

https://www.islamweb.net/ar/fatwa/183329/

Chapter Three
Full Delay

"The Fuqahaa' (Scholars) call the increase, when equality is demanded as Riba Al-Fadl, and the delay where immediate exchange is demanded, is called Riba Al-Nasaa'. These two types are particular to Riba Al-Buyu' (Sales)."

Sheikh Muhammad Abu Zahra

"Buhuth fi Al-Riba"

I. If the intention is receiving change, and the change is delayed fully

IN the first case, the example is of someone entering a shop and asking for change, and the manager does not have the change necessary, so he asks the man to return later to receive change for his money.

One view is that this is not acceptable. This view, is held by The Senior Council of Scholars of Saudi Arabia:

> **"Question: A man has 500 Riyals and needs change, but only finds 300 Riyals of change from the owner of the convenience store, and will take the rest later. Someone objected and said this is a type of Riba..."**

> **"Answer: It is not permissible for the two parties to a Sarf contract to separate except after receiving each, their full amounts, therefore it is not permissible for the person who paid 500 Riyals**

to take 300 Riyals immediately, and the rest after separation, even for a short time." (1)

The signatories on the above fatwa were: Sheikh Bakr Abu-Zaid, Sheikh Saleh Al-Fawzan, Sheikh Abdullah Ghudayyan, Sheikh Abdulrazzaq Afifi, and Sheikh Abdulaziz bin baz.

The Committee had made a similar fatwa on the above, Fatwa (14294), on page 458 of the same book above.

Although this fatwa relates to partial lack of exchange, it is the same ruling by The Committee for full or partial delay of change.

Sheikh Abdulkareem Al-Khudair, a member of the Permanent Committee and of the Senior Council of Scholars, is also of the same opinion:

> **"But if you come to the store owner and say I need change for this Ten, give me Two fives, and he said I only have a Five, so take Five and a Five will remain, this is not permissible, as this is the Sarf where delay (Nasaa') is not allowed." (2)**

Sheikh Muhammad bin Salih Al-Uthaimeen also has given his Fatwa on this issue when he was asked the question:

> **"Question: ...There are many who wishing to receive change for 50 Riyals goes to the seller and takes 30 Riyals, and the store owner promises to give him the rest in a few hours, so he gives him 50 and takes 30, and the rest remains the debt of the store owner for hours..."**

> **Answer: If he wants change for 50 Riyals, he must receive the change in the Majlis (session of contract) before they separate, and hands over the 50, so if possession is delayed from both sides, or from one side, this is Riba, whether the compensation is delayed in all or some, and this type is of Riba Al-Nasee'a (delay)..." (3)**

Sheikh Abdulaziz Al-Teraify also sees this type of case as Sarf, where the person did not purchase anything but simply wants change:

> **"If he wants change to purchase something, from a nearby store or far away, then it is not permissible unless there is Taqabud (immediate exchange), so he (the seller) cannot say "I will give you some of the change and the rest later", it must be hand to hand."** (4)

Sheikh Muhammad Al-Mukhtar Al-Shanqiti also explained this point:

> **"...For example, you have 500 Riyals for which you want change in hundreds or fifties, so you ask a man, and he says he would, but he doesn't have it right now but in an hour, and you both separate, the Sarf is voided, and he must return the 500 to you, and if you were to receive your 500 in change the next day, then the Riba that has been forbidden by Allah and his Messenger has occurred, and the taker and the giver are cursed..."** (5)

Another scholar who views any delay is forbidden is Sheikh Muhammad bin Ibrahim Al-Tuwaijri:

> **"The two parties to Sarf cannot separate unless both receive their full dues.**
>
> **If someone wants to change 100 Riyals, and he does not find in the store except 70 Riyals, he cannot take what is available, and leave the rest to be taken later, as this is Riba, as the Sale and Sarf of currencies must have immediate exchange in Majlis Al-Aqd (session of contract)."** (6)

Another group of scholars view that immediate exchange (Taqabud) is not necessary, however, they view close enough to immediate exchange is acceptable, as they view this as a middle ground. This is called "Hulool", which is simply longer than immediate exchange, and more defined as proximity of time (but not very long).

two scholars mentioned by Dr. Al-Mohaimeed are Sheikh Abdulrahman Al-Saa'di, and Dr. Yusuf Al-Shubaily who stated:

"...This is the issue of "Fakkah" as known in common language, for example a person has 100 Riyals and wants change, so he goes into a store and asks the seller for change, or buys something from the store, something simple such as a pop drink or sweets, or others, and what remains for example is 90 Saudi Riyals, and so the store owner goes somewhere else to get some change. You see now, either he gives back full change, or he buys for 10 Riyals and he gives him back 90 Riyals.

This is an exchange (Mubadalah) of two Ribawi items of the same kind, Riyals against Riyals. Thus Taqabud (immediate exchange), and Tamathul (equality), are both demanded. So if he (the store owner) went to another store to get change, or a nearby station, is this permissible?

There is a dispute between modern scholars, such as Sheikh Ibn Baz (Rahimahu Allah) who view this as forbidden since there was no Taqabud, because it is a Musarafah (Sarf) of a Ribawi item against another Ribawi item of the same kind, and Taqabud did not take place.

It is true there was Hulool, but there was no Taqabud.

Sheikh Abdulrahman Al-Sa'adi (Rahimahu Allah) had chosen a middle path and said that in such transactions Hulool is a requirement but not Taqabud. Meaning it is not permissible to delay it, as he can't take the one hundred Riyals and say: "I will give you the "Fakkah" tomorrow". If he delays it then the condition of Hulool is lost.

He (Sheikh Al-Sa'adi) stated that: "Taqabud is forgiven in this situation. It is permissible for him (the seller) to say: I shall go to that store to get you change, or go to another place to get change

and return it to you. He stated that this was a difficult situation to avoid, and happens often."

Perhaps, what Sheikh Abdulrahman Al-Sa'adi aimed for, was a middle solution." (7)

A third group of scholars do not view this as a contract of Sarf, but view money changing as a contract of Irfaq (benevolence), closer to a Qard, and thus the rule of Sarf demanding immediate exchange (Taqabud) or even close time exchange (Hulool) do not apply.

A question was asked of Sheikh Abdullah Ibn Jebreen also:

"Question: When a man buys an item for 50 Riyals, and gives the seller 100, and the seller does not have change, and says: come back tomorrow and I will give you the rest, is this permissible?

Answer: Permissible. This is one currency, and it is not called Sarf if the currencies are of the same type, because these denominations, the 50, the 100, the 200, are all one type, and one currency...Where separation is not allowed, is when the currencies are different, for example if you exchange Saudi Riyals against Yemeni or Qatari Riyals, there must be immediate exchange (Taqabud) before separation (of the parties)..." (8)

Sheikh Khalid Al-Mosleh on his website gives his opinion to a question asked:

"Question: Is it compulsory to change paper money simultaneously, and without any delay when changing similar currencies, or currencies for metals (coins)?"

Answer: The contemporary scholars have differed into three opinions regarding simultaneity and not delaying in changing similar currencies regardless of whether the currency being changed is of smaller denomination like changing a ten riyal note for ten one riyal notes, or two five riyal notes, and so on, or changing the currency to mineral coins of a similar value.

First opinion: It is compulsory to achieve simultaneity and proximity when changing paper currencies of a similar nature, changing minerals for minerals, or paper currency for minerals. This is the opinion of the majority.

Secondly: Simultaneity and proximity are not compulsory in this issue, rather, it is permissible to delay.

Thirdly: Simultaneity (immediate exchange) and proximity are not compulsory in this issue. However, it is not permissible to delay in this issue. This was the opinion of Sheikh Al-Saa'di.

The closer opinion is that it is not compulsory to achieve simultaneity and proximity in this issue, and it is permissible to delay, Regardless of whether we view paper money as equivalent to gold and silver, as the majority state, or it takes the rulings of "Fuloos" as others state.

This does not prevent delay in the contract of "Fakkah", since this contract in all its aspects, when currencies are the same, is a contract of benevolence and goodness, and a contract of Mu'awadah (for profit compensatory exchange).

The event of Mubadalah between the contracting parties does not require Mu'awadah (for profit compensatory exchange), when it is not intended. The Qard (loan) as the scholars define it is giving of money to another who will benefit from it, and receiving its equivalent, and it is agreed that there can be delay although it is a Mubadalah, as there is an absence of the intention of profit (Mu'awadah). Changing money is a Mubadalah for benevolence, and it has no requirement for the rules of compensation, as contracts are by their meaning.

Saying it is a Sarf contract and the rules apply, although the intention is not there, creates hardships in people's dealings, which the Shari'ah tries to ease and eliminate, as Shari'ah does not

prohibit the public good, and nothing is prohibited except with a clear text (nass)…" (9)

This is an important point that needs elaboration, and we quote Dr Al-Mohaimeed again who explains the issue and similarity with Qard:

"The contract of "Fakkah" (changing denominations), even though it has an exchange (Mubadalah) of money against money, is not a Sarf contract, but a contract that is under the contract of Qard in reality, and its rulings, even if it has a different name, and takes the rulings of Qard that do not demand simultaneous or immediate exchange.

To explain further: The contract of Sarf (currency sale) demands two items that are different in characteristics or content, however, if the two are the same, then the contract is a Qard even though it is called a Bai' (sale), as it is not envisioned that one sells something for something exactly equivalent, as this is illogical, and thus, if this happens, then it is a Loan, even though it is called a Sale, since if the two items differ, then it means a Sale, even if it is called something else, and if the items are the same, then it means a Loan, even if it is called something else…" (10)

This point cannot be overemphasized. This contract does not involve a Sale in the classical sense of wishing to benefit from the sale for profit, but is a desire of one party to be of help to another, whereas Sarf is for the sake profit usually:

"According to Al-Fayoumi in "Al-Misbah Al-Muneer, Sarf is the benefit of quality in a Dirham over the Dirham. Sarf includes the reality of a Sale, which involves the exchange of an item from the hand of the seller to the hand of the buyer, and the price from the hand of the buyer to the hand of the seller. And the same for the benefit (inequality), as the contracting parties, usually, desire the benefit arising in the price against the quality of the priced item." (11)

Thus we have the view that the intention is not the usual "Mu'awadah" contract, but a contract of benevolence between parties.

References

(1) The Permanent Committee for Scholarly Research and Iftaa', The Senior Council of Scholars, (Riyadh: Dar Al-Asima, 1999), Fatwa (16247), Volume 13, p. 459.

(2) Sheikh Abdulkareem Al-Khudair, "Sharh Buloogh Al-Maraam", Kitab Al-Buyu', Section 83, Page 10, Al-Maktaba Al-Shamila Al-Hadeetha.

https://al-maktaba.org/book/31729/2243 - p1[1]

(3) Sheikh Muhammad bin Salih Al-Uthaimeen, "Majmou' Fatawa", (Riyadh: Dar Al-Thurayyah Publishing, 2010), Volume 29, Kitab Al-Riba, pp. 365-366, Dated: October 9, 1999.

(4) Sheikh Abdulaziz Al-Teraify, July 7, 2014.

https://www.youtube.com/watch?v=O1m6Oy5WQwY

(5) Sheikh Muhammad Al-Mukhtar Al-Shanqiti, "Sharh Zad Al-Mustaqni'", Bab Al-Riba wa Al-Sarf, Section 165, Page 2, Al-Maktaba Al-Shamila Al-Hadeetha.

https://al-maktaba.org/book/32577/2976 - p1[2]

(6) Sheikh Muhammad bin Ibrahim Al-Tuwaijri, "Mawsu'at Al-Fiqh Al-Islami", (2009), Volume 3, Al-Riba, p. 489.

(7) Dr. Yusuf Al-Shubaily, "Fiqh Al-Mu'amalat Al-Masrafiyyah", 2006, (written from audiotapes by www.shamela.ws), pp. 67-68.

(8) Sheikh Abdullah Ibn Jebreen.

https://www.ibn-jebreen.com/books/1-223-8705-7595-32835.html

(9) Sheikh Khalid bin Abdullah Al-Mosleh, January 2, 2014.

https://almosleh.com/ar/16946

---

1. https://al-maktaba.org/book/31729/2243#p1

2. https://al-maktaba.org/book/32577/2976#p1

10) Dr. Muhammad Al-Mohaimeed, 'Ahkam Fakk Al-Nuqud", 2012, p. 21.

http://almohaimeed.net/up/book/alnqod.pdf

11) Dr. Abbas Ahmad Al-Baz, "Ahkam Sarf Al-Nuqud wa Al-Umlat", (Amman: Dar Al-Nafa'es, 1999), p. 16.

Chapter Four
Partial Delay

"They have been forbidden to engage in Riba Al-Fadl (Inequality) for fear of arriving at Riba Al-Nasee'a, because if they sold one Dirham for two…they would slowly move from immediate profit to a profit in delay in the exchange, and this is the heart of Riba Al-Nasee'a." (Delay and Increase)."

Ibn Al-Qayyim

"A'alam Al-Muwaqi'in"

I. <u>If the intention is receiving change, and the change is delayed partially</u>

PARTIAL receipt of change also has a dispute, along similar lines, where som state that if one doesn't receive their whole change then the whole deal is corrup and others state that only the part where no receipt was done is corrupt, as Ib Qudamah (Died Hijri 620) of the Hanbalis states in "Al-Muqne'":

"And if the two parties to Sarf separate before possession, or separate from the Majlis in a Salam transaction, even if some is received then they separate, it is corrupted in the whole deal, and this is one of two opinions, and the other opinion is that it is only corrupted in the part that has not been received…" (1)

But in his other book, a longer and more detailed explanation is written on Sar Ibn Qudamah elaborates on the issue of corruption of the contract. He states a others have, that whilst the contract is voided in the part of the change wher

here was no mutual possession, any extra that one of the parties received is
onsidered Amanah (on trust):

> "And if a man wants to exchange 1 Dinar for 10 Dirhams, but
> only has five, they cannot separate before possession of the whole
> 10 Dirhams, if he takes 5 Dirhams and they separate, the Sarf
> is voided in the half Dinar...But if he needs a solution, they can
> cancel the Sarf in the half of the deal not exchanged, or cancel the
> whole deal. He can then buy the Half Dinar for 5 Dirhams, pay
> it to the other, receive the whole 1 Dinar, the part that he bought
> (half) is his, and the other is an Amanah (trust) in his hands..." (2)

We saw in Chapter Two, that The Senior Council of Scholars of Saudi Arabia
rejects this as forbidden, whether it is full delay or partial delay:

> "Question: A man has 500 Riyals and needs change, but only finds
> 300 Riyals of change from the owner of the convenience store, and
> will take the rest later. Someone objected and said this is a type of
> Riba..."

> "Answer: It is not permissible for the two parties to a Sarf contract
> to separate except after receiving each, their full amounts,
> therefore it is not permissible for the person who paid 500 Riyals
> to take 300 Riyals immediately, and the rest after separation, even
> for a short time." (3)

Dr. Suleiman bin Fahd Al-Eissa, Professor of Higher Studies, Imam Muhammad
University, Saudi Arabia, also rejects partial receipt of change:

> "Question: A man was told by the storeowner that he did not have
> change, so he went to the store next door, to get change for 500
> Riyals. The storeowner said he only had 400 Riyals, take it and buy
> what you need, and return in half an hour and I will give you back
> your remaining hundred."

"Answer: ...It is known that most dealings these days are in paper money, which is a replacement for gold and silver, and has the same rulings of gold and silver. Based on this, when changing 500 Riyals, there must be immediate exchange and possession from both sides within the Majlis (session of contract), and it is not permissible to take some and delay some..." (4)

Sheikh Abi AbdulMu'iz Ferkous of Algeria forbids any delay in such a transaction and states his opinion to the question asked:

"Question: May I deal with customers in Sarf, where I receive 1,000 Algerian Dinars but I only have 750 Dinars in change at that time, and the client says: just give me what you have, and I'll come back for the rest later. Is this permissible?"

"Answer: Receiving some of the money, and delaying the rest until after separation (of the parties), even for a short time, is not permissible in Shari'ah, because of the absence of immediate exchange and possession in the Majlis (session of contract), which is a demanded condition in the contract of Sarf, and non-fulfillment of this condition makes this a Riba contract of the forbidden Riba of Sales..." (5)

Dr. Sa'ad Al-Khathlan, professor of Fiqh at Imam Muhammad University, Riyadh; was asked this question concerning partial receipt of change:

"Question: Sometimes I need change for, say 500 Riyals, and I find someone who can give me only 400 Riyals, and the rest later, is this permissible?"

Answer: "This transaction is a matter of dispute between scholars. Some have forbidden it, as you did not receive all your change, and paper money is similar to gold and silver, where it is demanded to have Equality (Tamathul), and Immediate Exchange (Taqabud).

Some view it as permissible if you consider that Sarf has taken place only in the amount you received, in this case, 400 Riyals, and the rest, 100 Riyals, is held in Trust (Amanah), or as Custody (Wadee'a) by the other person, and this to me is closer to the right ruling." (6)

Ibn Qudamah has an interesting take on this issue of partial Sarf, mentioned by some modern scholars as well. To avoid the pitfall of having a corrupted Sarf, both counterparts must be exchanged immediately, but if there is some amount outstanding then it becomes corrupt and is voided, thus it requires a solution for the remainder.

Ibn Qudamah in his "Al-Mughni" discusses a situation where there is an exchange of 1 Dinar against 10 Dirhams, which was the rate at the time:

"...And if one of them only had 5 Dirhams, and he buys a Half a Dinar, but he receives a whole Dinar, and has paid the other person the Dirhams, then he borrows them (the 5 Dirhams), and buys the other half of a Dinar, or buys the whole 1 Dinar against 10 Dirhams from the beginning, and pays the other person the 5 Dirhams, then borrows it, and then pays it back against the other half (of a Dinar), but without trickery, then it is permissible." (7)

So here, we have a method of achieving immediate exchange of the full amount, by borrowing what has been paid, to pay it again against the remainder, thus the act of Sarf is complete, and what remains outstanding is simply a Qard from one to another.

This was in fact mentioned by Sheikh Abdulaziz bin Baz (Rahimahu Allah), former Mufti of Saudi Arabia, and Head of The Senior Council of Scholars:

"Question: I work in a store, and my neighbor asks me to give him change for 50 Riyals and I only have 30, and he says: take the 50 and give me the 30, and you owe me 20. Is this permissible?"

"Answer: This is not permissible, because it has possession of some and delay of some, and Sarf must be hand to hand, the safe way is to give him the 50 on trust (Amanah), and take the 30 as Qard (loan), then they can settle the loan and is given the 50..." (8)

Full or partial receipt of your change is a minor issue compared to the bigger question and problem at hand. Those who view it as being a Sarf contract and make no difference between the same or different currencies regard immediate possession as a condition of validity, based upon the Hadith, and thus, any delay is Riba.

Those who view it as a Mubadalah contract where simply larger notes are exchanged for smaller notes do not regard it as Sarf, and for them the rules of Sarf do not apply. They regard it closer to Qard, a contract of benevolence and goodness, and do not regard delay as representing Riba.

Dr. Al-Mohaimeed explains:

"The majority of modern scholars have rules that getting change is a contract of Sarf, and the rules of Sarf apply.

The other view is that it is not Sarf, and it is a new contract that has not been named before, a new contract.

Thus we try to find the nearest old and known contract, whose rulings are known, we see which one is the closest in similarity and attach this new contract to it.

This contract of "Fakkah" is between the contract of Sarf and the contract of Qard. In all these three contracts, Fakkah, Sarf, and Qard, is an exchange (Mubadalah) of money for money.

In the Qard, it is based on delay, and the lender is rewarded for his actions (by Allah). So these contracts are similar, but the intentions are different.

In the Sarf contract, the intention is profit, and in the contract of Qard, the intention is benevolence...and in the contract of "Fakkah", the intention is benevolence, so to which of the contracts should we attach this new contract, to the contract of Bai' (Sale), meaning Sarf, or to the contract of Qard?

The Qard, because it agrees with it in areas: Mubadalah of money against money, delay, and the intention of benevolence. As such, the Qiyas (analogy) of the contract of "Fakkah" against Qard is more appropriate than the analogy with Sarf. Therefore we say, just as delay in money is permissible and is the basis of Qard, it is also permissible in "Fakkah"." (9)

But what if the intention were to purchase something and there were not enough change?

Would the rulings be different?

We shall see this in the next chapter.

References

(1) Ibn Qudamah, "Al-Muqne'", (Jeddah: Maktabat Al-Sawadi, 2000), Ba[b] Al-Riba wa Al-Sarf, p. 169.

(2) Ibn Qudamah, "Al-Mughni", (Riyadh: Dar Alam Al-Kutub, 1997), Volum[e] 6, p. 114.

(3) The Permanent Committee for Scholarly Research and Ifta', The Seni[or] Council of Scholars, (Riyadh: Dar Al-Asima, 1999), Fatwa (16247), Volume 1[?] p. 459.

(4) Dr. Suleiman bin Fahd Al-Eissa, August 21, 2003. Sections 9/70-71.

http://islamport.com/l/ftw/3893/4158.htm ¹

http://islamport.com/l/ftw/3893/4159.htm²

(5) Sheikh Abi AbdulMu'iz Ferkous, Algeria, September 24, 2010.

https://ferkous.com/home/?q=fatwa-1072

(6) Dr. Sa'ad Al-Khathlan, February 25, 2016.

http://saadalkhathlan.com/45

(7) Ibn Qudamah, "Al-Mughni", (Riyadh: Dar Alam Al-Kutub, 1997), Volum[e] 6, p. 114.

(8) Sheikh Abdulaziz bin Baz, "Fatawa Nour Ala Darb", (Riyadh: The Permane[nt] Committee for Scholarly Research and Ifta', 2011), Volume 19, pp. 148-149.

(9) Dr. Muhammad Al-Mohaimeed, February 21, 2017.

https://www.youtube.com/watch?v=yhgGXiAfiZs

---

1. http://islamport.com/l/ftw/3893/4158.htm%20%250D%250Dhttp://islamport.com/l/ftw/3893/4159.ht[m]

2. http://islamport.com/l/ftw/3893/4158.htm%20%250D%250Dhttp://islamport.com/l/ftw/3893/4159.ht[m]

Chapter Five
If The Intention Is A Sale

What distinguishes between this behavior and that behavior is the purpose and intent.

Ibn Taymiyyah

"Al-Fatawa Al-Kubra"

I. If the intention is a Sale, and the change is delayed

IF the intention is a sale, then you will find the rulings have changed, when intentions change, then rulings change, and the name of the contract changes as Ibn Taymiyyah stated:

"**What distinguishes between this behavior and that behavior is the purpose and intent. Without the Maqasid (purposes) and Niyah (intentions) of the people, the rulings would not change, and the names (of contracts) follow the Maqasid, and no one is allowed to think that the rulings have changed simply because of the change in names, whose meanings and purposes have not altered.**

When the Maqasid have changed with these actions, then the names and rulings differ. The Maqasid (purposes of contracts) are the reality of actions and their basis, and actions are judged by intent." (1)

The Permanent Committee of Saudi Arabia was asked a question on this particular issue and has answered that a delay in returning the change was not Riba, if the intention and action were based on a purchase:

"Question: I am a storeowner, and I have experienced a problem in my sales, which is that sometimes, when a person buys from me and gives me the amount, there is some remainder owed to him, and if I do not have any Sarf (change), he would say: I will come back tomorrow for my change...some have told me this is Riba..."

"Answer: Nothing in keeping some change behind by the purchaser with the seller, has an aspect of Riba. This is a contract of Bai' (Sale) and trusting the seller for the rest of the amount, and this is not a contract of Sarf." (2)

You will recall from Chapter Three, that in answer to the question of asking for change, the same committee stated that if change was what was demanded, then any delay of receiving the change is Riba, as it was a contract of Sarf.

Here, as the intention has changed to a Sale contract, then the rulings have changed, and delay is permissible.

Sheikh Muhammad bin Salih Al-Uthaimeen answered this when questioned about a man receiving change with delay. You will recall from Chapter Three that the Sheikh was asked whether in Sarf, the change could be delayed and his answer was in the negative, as this was Riba.

This was the answer when the intention of the person was to actually only get change. However in the same question, the Sheikh was also asked:

Question: "...Would the ruling be the same if the person bought from the store owner and some change remained as debt with the seller?

Answer: "It does not enter into this ruling, if he bought something and he gave the seller more than the price, the excess can remain with the seller as a Qard (Loan), or Wadee'a (Custody)." (3)

Sheikh Suleiman Al-Rehaily was asked the question concerning buying an item and not receiving the rest of the change until another day. He states:

"If I bought an item worth 70 Dirhams and I paid 100 Dirhams, and the seller does not have 30 Dirhams, and he asks me to return tomorrow to get the rest of my money, is there an issue? Some scholars say this is not permissible as it is Sarf...and nothing must remain in debt. Others say it is permissible as it is not Sarf, not in reality nor in custom, since the motive of the payer is not Sarf, neither is the motive of the seller to do Sarf, thus it is a fulfillment of rights." (4)

Sheikh Abdulmohsin Al-Zamil agrees with Sheikh Al-Rehaily, and states that this is not of Sarf, also called Musarafah, but is a sale and the remainder can be delayed, as it would be fulfillment of the rights of the buyer. He was asked a question regarding buying an item where the change would be delayed:

"This issue is when you buy an item, and your purchase was not a Hila (trick) to perform Sarf...For example he buys an item that is insignificant, for one Riyal for example, for the purpose of receiving change, and so he receives some change and leaves behind some change. This is a trick. But if he intended to make a purchase, even if it is of a small price, and he does not find available all the change, this is not called Musarafah, this is Wafaa' (fulfillment of rights).

When you buy from the store an item, say for 10 Riyals and you give him 100 Riyals, the reality is that your right in this amount is 90 Riyals, so you are not performing Musarafah, as Musarafah is 100 against 100. Thus, this is Wafaa' or Istifaa' (fulfillment of rights), and Istifaa' has a different ruling than Sarf." (5)

Other scholars also agree, such as Sheikh Zaid bin Musfir Al-Bahri, who points out that there is a difference if it were pure Sarf where the person intended to simply have change for the money.

> "If I go to the store and ask the owner to give me change for a 100, and he says he has only 90 or 99, this is not permissible, since there was no Qabd (possession) before separation, but when I go to the store and buy something, and some change remains with the store owner, there is no issue, why? Because there was no purchase of a Ribawi against Ribawi, as I bought from him, and did not perform Sarf." (6)

Sheikh Abdulaziz Al-Teraify also sees this case as a purchase and not a Sarf:

> "Some scholars qualify this as a Sarf, but it seems to me not a Sarf, it is a contract of the group of contracts of Sale, and the remainder (with the store owner) is considered Debt." (7)

Others such as Sheikh Suleiman Al-Majid see no problem if it were a purchase since the Sarf was not intended but the purchase was, but if it were a Sarf, then any delay would be Riba.

> "If it were pure Sarf, for example I need change for 100 Riyals, can I take 50 now and the leave the rest until later, this is not permissible, because Sarf is intended as opposed to a Sale, so when you buy with 100, and the seller only has 50 change to give back, and the rest delayed until later, here the intention is a Sale and not Sarf." (8)

And others such as Sheikh Abdullah bin Nasser Al-Salmi view no problem in delay if it is a sale, since when it is a sale, it is no longer Sarf, since the purchase was made for only part of the money, for example paying 10 Dirhams for an item worth 5 Dirhams, and 5 Dirhams then remain as change. The remainder has not been part of any 'Mu'awadah' contract, and can be delayed.

If however, it is a Sarf, where the person intentionally wants change for his money, then no delay is allowed, except that the remainder can be delayed if it is confirmed as an 'Amanah', and so it is removed from being a 'Mu'awadah' contract to an item held on trust with the other party.

"Question: I bought an item for 5 Riyals and I gave him (the seller) 10 Riyals, and he does not have change, so I left to return later?

Answer: This is not Sarf, for it to be said that this is Riba or not. Why? Because when someone gives the storeowner 10 Riyals, when he has bought for 5, the Mu'awadah contract is established on a part of the 10, which is the purchase.

The other 5 has had no transaction performed on it, so if the delivery of change is delayed or he says come back tomorrow, there is no issue. This is not Sarf, and what some have understood that this constitutes a Sarf, is wrong." (9)

heikh Abdulkareem Al-Khudair is also among those who view a purchase as ifferent from Sarf when he was asked the question about someone who leaves oney behind after a purchase when the storeowner does not have enough hange:

"No, this is not Riba, because you bought an item from the store, so you bought yoghurt for five, and he told you he does not have change and you had given him ten, he said leave the five until the afternoon." (10)

his of course is also supported by examples from classic Fiqh literature such as l-Hajjawi (Died Hijri 968) in his Al-Iqnaa':

"...And if he bought silver against one and a half Dinars, and paid to the seller 2 Dinars to take his due, even after separation (from the Majlis), it is permissible, and the extra is an Amanah (trust)..." (11)

is also mentioned by Ibn Rushd, the grandfather (Died 520 Hijri):

"And he was asked (meaning Malik) about a man who comes to the seller with a Dinar, and buys oil for a quarter, and dates for a quarter, and suwaiq (type of barley or wheat) for a quarter, and leaves behind a quarter. And he answered: there is no objection. Muhammad Ibn Rushd said: He permitted leaving behind a quarter of a Dinar...as Custody (Wadee'a)." (12)

Sheikh Muhammad bin Sa'ad Al-Osaimi, Professor at Umm Al-Qura University in Makkah, also has the same view but gives more elaboration on this type of transaction:

"This transaction is a price and a purchase, and has no contract of Sarf in it, and the remainder is what is left after the purchase and is allowed to be delayed, and it is not an exchange (Mubadalah) of money against money for it to be Sarf.

The intended is the item, and not Sarf, and intentions have their effect on transactions. The picture may look the same, and the rulings differ, just as it is in the exchange of Dirham for Dirham with delay. If the intention is Mu'awadah (compensatory exchange), then it is forbidden, but if the intention is benevolence, it is permissible.

The remainder stays with the seller as Amanah, just as when a buyer takes the merchandise and doesn't pay, it becomes a debt owed by him, and debt is an Amanah.

Some may say, this is not allowed because it is a sale of a Ribawi item against another item with a Ribawi item included, but this is not necessarily the rule in the school.

And the Wadee'a, if permission is given to use, becomes a Qard (loan), and the remainder of the change was authorized to be dealt with, so it is as if he bought from him and he loaned him, which is not forbidden." (13)

Among those who disagree is Sheikh Muhammad Al-Shanqiti, who views any delay, whether it was a purchase mainly or Sarf mainly as the same:

"One of the mistakes that people make, for example, is if you bought a book for 10 Riyals and you gave him 100 Riyals, you have two contracts...every small or large issue has its rulings in Shari'ah, so if you have given him 100 Riyals to take from it 10, that means you bought the book for 10, and he will give you 90 against the 90, so the issue of the book is not a problem, the problem is with the 90, and what applies to it are the rules of Sarf, thus he has to give you 90 against 90 with no addition or subtraction. And possession must take place before separation, so if you left the store, or he left the store, then Riba Al-Nasee'a has taken place." (14)

It would seem the majority are of the view that when the intention is to buy an item, then the contract has moved from being one of the exchange of money against money, to a sale contract, with a different ruling.

This implies that the remainder of the change does not fall under any rules of Sarf, and it is simply a fulfillment of rights for the buyer. It can be considered a type of Amanah, or even Qard, which is effectively a debt owed by the storeowner.

Others, mainly Sheikh Al-Shanqiti, see no difference and split the picture into two contracts, one in which the item was purchased and money was given against it, which is no problem. The other, meaning the remainder of the change is effectively a second contract, and that is an exchange of money against money and the rules of Sarf apply and thus any delay is forbidden.

But what happens if the intention were to get change, but this intention were not declared and the person buys something only for the sake of getting change for his money?

Do rulings differ?

We shall see in the next chapter.

References

(1) Ibn Taymiyyah, "Al-Fatawa Al-Kubra", (Beirut: Dar Al-Kotob Al-Ilmiyah 1987), Volume 6, p. 61.

(2) The Permanent Committee for Scholarly Research and Ifta', The Senior Council of Scholars, (Riyadh: Dar Al-Asima, 1999), Fatwa (18203), Volume 13 pp. 180-181.

(3) Sheikh Muhammad bin Salih Al-Uthaimeen, "Majmou Fatawa", (Riyadh Dar Al-Thurayyah Publishing, 2010), Volume 29, Kitab Al-Riba, pp. 365-366 Dated: October 9, 1999.

(4) Sheikh Suleiman Al-Rehaily, "Dawabit Al-Riba", (Sharjah: Islamic Affair Department, 2015), pp. 210-211.

(5) Sheikh Abdulmohsin Al-Zamil, May 2, 2015.

https://www.youtube.com/watch?v=3M8_t4URcc0

(6) Sheikh Zaid bin Musfir Al-Bahri, December 2, 2015.

https://www.youtube.com/watch?v=gZMDPv87lV0

(7) Sheikh Abdulaziz Al-Teraify, July 7, 2014.

https://www.youtube.com/watch?v=O1m6Oy5WQwY

(8) Sheikh Suleiman Al-Majid, February 21, 2016.

https://www.youtube.com/watch?v=6cfnCCNMe8Y

(9) Sheikh Abdullah bin Nasser Al-Salmi, January 20, 2016.

https://www.youtube.com/watch?v=barkySHxoAE

(10) Sheikh Abdulkareem Al-Khudair, "Sharh Buloogh Al-Maraam", Kitab Al-Buyu', Section 83, Page 10, Al-Maktaba Al-Shamila Al-Hadeetha.

https://al-maktaba.org/book/31729/2243 - p1[1]

11) Al-Hajjawi, "Al-Iqnaa'", (Beirut: Dar El-Marefa), Volume 2, p. 122.

12) Ibn Rushd (The Grandfather), "Al-Bayan wa Al-Tahsil", (Beirut: Dar Al-Gharb Al-Islami, 1984), Volume 6, p. 444.

13) Sheikh Muhammad bin Sa'ad Al-Osaimi, June 1st, 2015.

https://dmohamadsaad.tumblr.com/post/122070876000

14) Sheikh Muhammad Al-Mukhtar Al-Shanqiti, "Sharh Zad Al-Mustaqni'", Bab Al-Riba wa Al-Sarf, Section 165, Page 3, Al-Maktaba Al-Shamila Al-Hadeetha.

https://al-maktaba.org/book/32577/2977 - p1[2]

---

1. https://al-maktaba.org/book/31729/2243#p1

2. https://al-maktaba.org/book/32577/2977#p1

Chapter Six
Declaration To The Seller, Inequality, And Benefits

"I am afraid we might have exaggerated in Riba ten times for fear of it"

Umar Bin Al-Khattab (RAA)

"Musannaf Ibn Abi Shayba"

IV. <u>If the intention is receiving change and an item is purchased, without declaration to the seller, and the change is delayed</u>

FOR some scholars, the intention is important, as it would change the ruling from permissible to forbidden.

This is where someone wants change for their money, but perhaps feels that the owner of a store would not be helpful unless he purchased something, so he enters the store and purchases an item with for a small amount and gives the owner a large note, hoping to get some change, but of course without informing the owner of his intention. Everybody might have done this at some point.

In this case, if the owner does not have enough change and the money has to be delayed, what is the ruling?

For some scholars like Sheikh Walid Rashed Al-Saedan, it's all about intention:

"There are three views on this from scholars. Some say it is permissible absolutely, and some say it is forbidden absolutely, while some have given details and took a middle view on this issue.

They said that it would depend on your intention. If you intended to purchase, then what change remains with the seller, is not considered part of a transaction of Sarf, but a type of Amanah (trust) left behind and it is permissible, since you did not enter to perform Sarf, but entered to purchase.

But some people for example may have 500 Riyals and they know they would not receive change from the owner of the store unless they purchase something, so he hides the intention of Sarf and reveals the intention of purchase, so he uses the purchase as a cover for his intentions, and the meaning of contracts is in their intentions and not what is revealed, and in this case and with this intention, it is not permissible to keep any change with the seller, as this transaction is Sarf, based on your intention, and the rules are that there must be equality (Tamathul) and immediate exchange (Taqabud), so we cannot say it is forbidden absolutely nor permissible absolutely, but it depends on your intentions." (1)

Sheikh Abdulmohsin Al-Zamil was asked about someone who purchased an item and the seller did not have enough change. Sheikh Al-Zamil already approved the delay of the change if it is a true purchase, as it is not Sarf, but a fulfillment of rights.

On the other hand, he said:

"That is unless your purchase is a Hila (trick) of Sarf. So it has different aspects, the first scenario is that the purchase is a trick to transact in Sarf (meaning you only bought to get change), so he needs to get change and he buys an item, which is worth little, like one Riyal, so that he can get change, so gets back some and leaves some, but this is a trick." (2)

This case is of course problematic, as intentions are hidden, so only the person would know if that were the intention. One might say that if the note is of a large denomination, and the amount purchased is very small, then it is a clear case of undeclared intentions, but the reality is that one never knows.

V. <u>If the intention is receiving change, and it is declared to the seller, and an item is included against the remaining change</u>

What if instead of being asked to delay the change, the person who declares he wants change for his money, is asked to include an item to be purchased covering the remaining amount of change?

If on the other hand, one has the intention to only get change, but is asked to take an item instead against the rest of the change owed, then it's a different case.

Sheikh Al-Shanqiti states that if a person asks for change and the seller does not have enough change but offers an item instead with the remaining, then this is a problem, since it must be assumed there is a profit element in the item.

As such, the person for example gave 100, and received 90 in change, and was given an item for 10 instead, there would be a profit in it, say 1 Dirham, and as such, the exchange took place between 100 and 99. This is Riba Al-Fadl where items are exchanged unequally, where equality is demanded. If however, it were a sale, then it is acceptable since the Sarf part follows the sale, and profit in a sale is acceptable.

> **"If he says to him: I do not have change, but I have 90 Riyals and I have an item for 10 Riyals or for 20 Riyals. It may appear at first that he is giving him 80 Riyals and an item worth 20 Riyals, it may appear that this permissible, since the total is now 100.**
>
> **But this is a problem, and is suspect, since the item for 10 or for 20 is not sold unless there is a profit, so the item for 10 is actually for 9, otherwise why would he sell it, he would only sell if there is a profit, so it is as if he is saying: I will give you change and I will take a profit, and this is a Mustafdil (a person who has taken a difference in an exchange).**
>
> **Based upon this, it is as if he has given change (Sarf) of 100 for less. Some scholars may, in a hurry, approve it, but the problem in it, as some scholars have stated, is in the contract of sale, by including it in a Sarf contract, that one is not secure that there exists a benefit**

to the seller given the presence of profit in the sold item, since the majority of sales are based on taking profit.

It is best to stay clear of a Sarf contract where a purchase is obligated." (3)

his actually happens a lot, in many supermarkets, especially where the change ometimes is very small and there is no coinage to reimburse the purchaser, and an item is inserted, such as a piece of gum.

some stores, they began to record it down and collect these small amounts eople leave behind, and then on a regular basis, give it to charity. That of course a very good idea. I have done this myself in a supermarket in Saudi Arabia.

VI. <u>If the intention is to receive change but where there is inequality between the amounts due to a fee or a benefit</u>

nd the next case is where the person providing the change, wishes to take omething for themselves for providing the service of change.

here is no dispute about this issue, that when exchanging money for money or the sake of getting change, that if it is paper against paper or metal against netal (coins), that no difference in the amounts should take place, this is called afadul (Inequality), and is strictly prohibited as part of the Riba of Sales (Riba l-Buyu').

ou will of course recall the Hadith from Part 1 related from Ubada bin Al-Samit oncerning the six Ribawi species and the rules of sale. Ibn Al-Munther (Died Iijri 318) relates the consensus (Ijmaa'):

"They have agreed that the six species, in Inequality, exchanged hand to hand, or with Delay, is not permissible, against themselves, it is forbidden." (4)

)r. Al-Mohaimeed elaborates on this last point:

"I do not know of any dispute between modern scholars as to the lack of permissibility of inequality if the change is between paper money against paper money, or metal money (coins) against metal money, as it was the school of our earlier scholars to forbid inequality between a Ribawi item against its own kind.

Therefore, it is forbidden to provide change with inequality, whether the inequality was in money or a benefit.

An example of money: Zaid gives Amr a piece of 100 Riyals to get some change, and Zaid stipulates that he would only do that if he gets something and gives back for example only 99 Riyals.

An example of benefit: This is where the seller agrees to giving change but stipulates that the person buys something from him or offers him a service." (5)

This is also a problematic issue, since the unwillingness of the seller to give change unless one buys from the store is not always declared but understood.

In such cases therefore, was it a purchase or a forbidden benefit of the Mubadalah? How would the storeowner know whether you are actually buying from him, or in fact only want change, but heard that he wouldn't unless you buy?

Part of this issue is the dispute sometimes seen in scholarly works that view the combination of a Bai' and Sarf as forbidden. Some regard these two contracts and others as having different rulings and can be contradictory, and as such they must not be combined.

Here's a statement from Ibn Qudamah from his work "Al-Kafi":

"If he combines two contracts with different rulings, such as a Bai' and Ijarah, or Sarf; with one price, it is permissible, since the different rulings do not endanger the permissibility, such as combining what has Preemption of Rights with what does not.

But there is another view; that it is not permissible, since their rulings are different, and neither is preferred over the other, and it is void in both. A Sale has an option (Khiyar) in it, and it is not mandatory to have Taqabud in the Majlis...But Sarf is required to have Taqabud..." (6)

But can the amounts be different if it were paper money against metal money (coins)?

This is what we will look at in the next chapter.

References

(1) Sheikh Walid Rashed Al-Saedan, April 13, 2017.

https://www.youtube.com/watch?v=-dJnsZk5lN8

(2) Sheikh Abdulmohsin Al-Zamil, May 2, 2015.

https://www.youtube.com/watch?v=3M8_t4URcc0

(3) Sheikh Muhammad Mukhtar Al-Shanqiti, November 9, 2012.

https://www.youtube.com/watch?v=QtkcwDR1Ycw

(4) Ibn Al-Munther, "Al-Ijmaa'", (Ajman: Maktabat Al-Furqan; Ras Al-Khaimah: Maktabat Makkah Al-Thaqafiah, 1999), Kitab Al-Buyu', Clause 547, p. 133.]

(5) [Dr. Muhammad Al-Mohaimeed, 'Ahkam Fakk Al-Nuqud", 2012, p. 38.

http://almohaimeed.net/up/book/alnqod.pdf

(6) Ibn Qudamah, "Al-Kafi", (Giza: Dar hajr, 1997), Volume 3, p. 50.

Chapter Seven
Paper Money And Metal Money

"Riba is one of the most confusing issues for Scholars."

Ibn Kathir

"Tafsir Ibn Kathir"

VII. <u>The unequal exchange between paper money and metal money (coins), is this permissible?</u>

HERE are some scholars who have approved of the Unequal exchange between paper money and metal coinage.

The Permanent Committee of the Senior Council of Scholars in Saudi Arabia, for example approved a difference between the exchange of paper money against metal coins:

"Question: I sell 9 Riyals of metal (coins) against 10 Riyals of paper, and I add some gum or miswak (piece of wood for cleaning teeth) on top?"

"Answer: ...There is no objection to Inequality in the Sarf of Saudi Paper Currency against Saudi Metal Currency, due to the difference in material, with the condition that an immediate exchange takes place in the Majlis (session of contract)." (1)

The members don't seem to have taken account of the fact that the seller is adding an item to the exchange. So this is a situation where he was asked for change, and perhaps he didn't have enough, so added something on top to equalize the matter. So it would look more like the case discussed before, but with a twist rather than a new situation.

But here, the committee did not respond to that but instead approved the exchange between monies with inequality based on them being different material.

It was perhaps felt that metal is a different genus, and thus one can have difference in quantity, although most scholars view both coins and paper as representing money and have the same "Illah" or characteristic, which is "Thamaniyyah", meaning they are values or prices of things and not due to what they are made of.

Sheikh Ibn Uthaimeen also views this as possible and has given his approval:

> **"The issue is the Sarf of Riyals of metal against Riyals of paper, is it permissible to have inequality?**
>
> **Modern scholars have differed. Some have said it was forbidden, as the metal Riyal is the same as the paper Riyal, there is no difference and the purpose is the same, and the government has made both their relative values equal.**
>
> **Others said it was permissible, because there is a difference between them, as the genus is different in reality and in value, and they are only equal because of the government. The proof is that if you had 100 kg of the metal and 100 kg of paper, are their values the same?**
>
> **The answer: It is different; the metal is bought for itself, while the paper, without the government consideration would be worthless.**
>
> **They said: when the genus is different, in reality and value, inequality in an exchange is permissible due to The Prophet's (PEACE BE UPON HIM) statement: "If the genera are different, sell as you wish, if hand to hand."**

Sheikh Ibn Baz, with The Permanent Committee had forbidden that, but the Sheikh said recently that he re-considered.

I myself, am comfortable with permissibility, and I have no doubts, and our Sheikh, Abdulrahman bin Sa'adi (Rahimahu Allah), permitted that..." (2)

Sheikh Ibn Baz did answer a question on this issue, which is part of his Fatawa book, in fact there are several questions concerning this issue, and they show an in between view, with more of a preference for equality.

The Sheikh was asked five questions in total on this issue, which shows the interest people have in this issue, and perhaps the level of confusion.

Here are some examples:

Example 1:

"Question: ...The store owner stipulates that any one who wants Sarf must either buy from the store or he would give 9 coins for a 10 Riyal note, what is the ruling on this?"

"Answer: The modern scholars have disputed on this issue. Some have allowed inequality and said: metal money is different from paper money, and therefore inequality (Tafadul) is permissible due to The Prophet's (PEACE BE UPON HIM) statement: "If the genera are different, sell as you wish", if hand to hand as is done between gold against silver, and a US Dollar against a Saudi Riyal, since one is different from the other; paper money is different from metal money.

Others have said, there must be equality, as this is a Riyal and the other is a Riyal, ten for ten, and a hundred for a hundred. It would be more prudent not to sell except with equality, taking into account "leaving what is suspicious for what is not suspicious", and to avoid the dispute between scholars." (3)

<u>Example 2:</u>

> **"Question: Can we buy 1,000 Riyals of coins, and then sell 9 coins against one 10 Riyal note, is this permissible?"**

> **"Answer: It is more prudent to have equality, but if it is done, then Allah willing, there is no problem, but it is more prudent to have equality...of paper and coins, because it is all called money..."** (3)

The only issue that was not answered, unfortunately, by Sheikh Ibn Baz, was the issue of when the storeowner stipulates a benefit to him, as was asked in a number of questions.

Sheikh Ibn Jebreen also approved of a difference between paper money and coin money when receiving change. He was asked about a case where people used to pay paper money to get coins to use for the telephone in those days:

> **"Question: Can one sell paper money against coins without equality, for example 9 one Riyal coins against one 10 Riyal paper note?**

> **"Answer: I see it permissible, due to the need for the use of coins in telephones, and since silver or metal coins are not available everywhere, and someone has to work to gather them. He may not find except in far away places such as institutions and banks, and it takes time, and costs of travel, and this is an expense, so he must be compensated for his effort. And it is also the case, that whilst it is mixed with other types of money, there is a difference in carrying, benefit, and perishability, and cancellation, and the Hadith states that if the genera are different, sell as you wish."** (4)

In the above answer to the question, there are in fact two distinct answers by Sheikh Ibn Jebreen: a) The difference in exchange due to taking a fee for work (Ujrah), and b) an exchange of money against money unequally due to difference in material, meaning paper against metal. The first would not be an issue as it is

ee for work done, the second however, would not probably receive consensus, as
hey are both considered national currencies of the same kind and amount.

The answer to those who permit a difference in exchange between metal coins
nd paper money, from other scholars can best be summarized by Dr.
Al-Mohaimeed's response in his paper on changing money:

> **"It is not accepted that it is a different genus based on the material
> of which it is made due to the following:**
>
> **Its value, if considered as one currency, is the same, and cannot
> change in any circumstances for the purpose of buying, selling, or
> settling debts.**
>
> **The true value of a currency is the number printed on it, and this
> mark is from the same kind and from the same country, whether
> imprinted on paper or metal.**
>
> **As for the material of paper or metal, it has no value in itself, and
> no weight in reality; its reality is that it contains that mark printed
> on it.**
>
> **The proof of that is that if the government cancelled the legal usage
> of a currency, that paper and metal will no longer have any value.**
>
> **If the paper and metal were to be sold without a mark of value
> imprinted on them, we may find that the one metal Riyal is worth
> more than even the paper that is a 500 Riyal note.**
>
> **Thus the differentiation based on the type of material, such as the
> difference in genus between gold and silver, or barley and wheat,
> is a differentiation without effective difference, especially among
> those who consider that current money is an independent money
> on its own just like gold and silver." (5)**

Other scholars who have disapproved of the unequal exchange between paper
money and coins is Dr. Abbas Ahmad Al-Baz, author of a book on Sarf:

"It is a widespread in some Islamic countries; the custom of exchanging a currency against a different denomination of the same currency in inequality.

If someone wanted to exchange paper for coins, the other party, the owner of the coins, discounts the number of coins to be exchanged as a fee. They do not consider this Riba, as they view paper money as one genus, and coins as an independent genus, and with this difference, equality is not demanded.

This action is incorrect, because reference to the Hadiths that dealt with the issue of Sarf demands absolute equality in the same genus...and modern currency is stand-alone money separate from gold and silver, and a country's currency is all one genus given the same issuing source, even if its picture and size differ.

The meaning is not in its material, but in its source of issuance, thus if the source of issuance of the paper and coins is one, it is forbidden to have inequality and immediate exchange is demanded.

A country produces paper for lightness of weight and ease of carry, and coins as a supplement for low value items, and is considered money by the government and individuals, and achieves the same purpose as paper, they both are used to purchase goods, and there is no room for differentiation as they are one genus.

If the intention is to take a fee for the exchange of paper against its own type, for example that it is a note of 10 Dinars, and its owner wanted to get change (coins) in what is called "Fakkah", then this is forbidden Riba, and this is not considered a fee, since a fee is only taken against some effort that is undertaken, and here there is no effort." (6)

Although some scholars have approved it, it would seem more and more scholar deem it incorrect to permit, as they see both metal and paper of the sam

rrency as the same genus, as declared in so few words in this fatwa from
uwait:

"Question: What is the ruling on exchanging paper money with the same currency, given that the person takes a fee for performing this exchange? For example, one takes a Dinar of paper money and gives its owner 900 Fils in coins, for using in the telephones...?"

"Answer: Not permissible, because of the inequality (Tafadul) between them given they are the same currency." (7)

his is also the opinion of AAOIFI, in its Shari'ah Standard No. 1 on Trading in
urrencies:

"2/1/2 The counter values of the same currency must be of equal amount, even if one of them is in paper money and the other is in coin of the same country, like a note of one pound for a coin of one pound." (8)

nother opinion is from the scholars of the popular website Islamweb.net, who
ere asked about a percentage taken when paper money is exchanged with metal
oney on public transport:

"It is not permissible to sell paper currency for a lesser amount of metal currency or other, as it is the same kind, and what is called "Fakkah", or "Tasreef", is in reality a sale, and at the time of Mubadalah (Exchange) when the currency is the same, are two conditions:

The first: Taqabud (immediate exchange) in the Majils (session of contract).

The second: Equality, no Tafadul (inequality).

The Prophet (PEACE BE UPON HIM) has said: {"Gold for gold, silver for silver, wheat for wheat, barley for barley, dates for dates, and salt for salt, like for like and equal for equal, hand to hand.

**If these classes differ, then sell as you wish if it is hand to hand."}
(Reported by Muslim).**

Paper and metal money perform the function of gold and silver in our time, because people have become accustomed to it, and they have become Athman (prices) of goods. " (9)

In Sudan also, the newspapers reported that The Islamic Fiqh Academy of Sudan has forbidden any difference in amounts between the same currencies whether paper or metal:

"The Islamic Fiqh Academy has clarified beyond doubt the issue by forbidding the selling of the same kind of currency and metal coins as "Fakkah" (change) in different prices.

And has stated that it is of the forbidden Riba. The Academy has stated that taking advantage of people's needs for smaller pieces is not a Sale but a forbidden Riba, and that currencies traded these days such as the Pound (Sudanese) are of the same stature as gold and silver and take their rulings of the demand for equality (Tamathul) and being hand to hand (Taqabud)." (10)

Of course, many scholars do not approve of anything less than absolute equality in these exchanges regardless of the material of the money itself, so I leave the last word to Sheikh Muhammad Al-Tuwaijri:

"He who exchanges Ten Riyals of paper money against nine of metal money (coins) is a "Murabi" (Riba Consumer), and both are partners in guilt." (11)

References

1) The Permanent Committee for Scholarly Research and Ifta', The Senior Council of Scholars, (Riyadh: Dar Al-Asima, 1999), Fatwa (18523), Volume 13, p. 457.

2) Sheikh Muhammad bin Salih Al-Uthaimeen, "Al-Sharh Al-Mumti'", (Al-Dammam: Dar Ibn Al-Jawzi, 2003), Volume 6, pp. 94-95.

3) Sheikh Abdulaziz bin Baz, "Fatawa Nour Ala Darb", (Riyadh: The Permanent Committee for Scholarly Research and Ifta', 2011), Volume 19, pp. 149-152.

4) Sheikh Abdullah bin Abdulrahman Al-Jebreen, Fatwa 8908.

http://cms.ibn-jebreen.com/fatwa/home/view/8908

5) Dr. Muhammad Al-Mohaimeed, 'Ahkam Fakk Al-Nuqud", 2012, p. 40.

http://almohaimeed.net/up/book/alnqod.pdf

6) Dr. Abbas Ahmad Al-Baz, "Ahkam Sarf Al-Nuqud wa Al-Umlat", (Amman: Dar Al-Nafa'es, 1999), pp. 175-176.

7) Majmou'at Al-Fatawa Al-Shari'yyah, Minsitry of Awqaf, Kuwait.

Fatwa # (2660), December 4, 2017.

http://www.fatawa.com/view/4039/

8) AAOIFI Shari'ah Standards 2017, Shari'ah Standard No. (1): Trading in Currencies, p. 52.

9) Islamweb.net, The Ruling on "Fakk Al-Nuqud" for a percentage, Fatwa 183329, 12 July 2012.

https://www.islamweb.net/ar/fatwa/183329/

10) Alnilin website, 21 August 2014.

https://www.alnilin.com/1085901.htm

(11) Sheikh Muhammad bin Ibrahim Al-Tuwaijri, "Mawsu'at Al-Fiqh Al-Islami" (2009), Volume 3, Al-Riba, p. 489.

Chapter Eight
Summary

"We find the (so-called) jurists of our times believing that the one who has memorized the most opinions has the greatest legal acumen.

Their view is like the view of one who thought that a cobbler is he who possesses a large number of shoes and not one who has the ability to make them.

It is obvious that the person who has a large number of shoes, will, (some day), be visited by one whose feet the shoes do not fit. He will then go back to the cobbler who will make shoes that are suitable for his feet. This is the position of most of the faqihs of these times."

Ibn Rushd

"The Distinguished Jurist's Primer"

MOST schools of jurisprudence call the act of selling money against money by the word Sarf. But there is a difference amongst schools. Whereas the three other schools call a transaction Sarf whenever two currencies are exchanged, whether they are different currencies or the same currency, the Maliki School only calls it Sarf if the currencies are different.

They use three main terms to denote different actions: 1) Sarf is when the currencies are different, such as gold against silver, 2) Muratalah, when it is gold against gold, or silver against silver being exchanged by weight, and 3) Mubadalah, when it is the same currency against itself, if the exchange is by numbers.

The transaction where a person needs smaller denomination notes or coins fo
a larger note is closer to Mubadalah. Modern scholars call this a contract o
"Fakkah", or "Fakk Al-Nuqud". In Arabic, "Fakk" is breaking up an item o
separating its parts. Nuqud of course is the plural of Naqd, which is money.

There is no dispute in history or today, that in a contract of Sarf, certain rule
must apply. These rules are that an exchange must have immediate mutua
possession (Taqabud), and when the currencies are the same, such as gold agains
gold, then another condition, is equality in values (Tamathul), evidenced in gol
and silver by equal weights.

This is agreed and based upon a Hadith that set out the rules of the exchang
of goods, both money and foods, in sales, and is part of what is known as Rib
Al-Buyu', or the Riba of Sales.

Paper money according to the vast majority of modern scholars has replaced gol
and silver, but the rules of Sarf apply equally to it as they do to metal coins.

Both Sarf and Qard (Loan), have commonalities, in that both involve a
exchange of money for money. In the case of Qard, delay is permitted, as that i
the basis of its benefit, as it is mainly a contract of benevolence, which is why n
return could be stipulated in it.

The issue for modern scholars was how to view this contract of Mubadalah o
"Fakkah" in comparison to existing contracts, so as to define the rulings tha
apply.

Since Mubadalah shares common traits with both Sarf and Qard, in the area o
the exchange of money for money, then, is there a characteristic that it share
more with one and not the other?

Yes, and that is the Intention.

The intention of a contract of Mubadalah is also benevolence, as the parties t
the transaction are not seeking profit, as they are in Sarf, but an act of help. Whe
one seeks to break up a large denomination note into smaller denomination
whose purpose is to be able to buy lower priced items, he is basically asking th
other party a favor.

his means that Mubadalah shares with Qard a very important characteristic that does not share with Sarf, and since delay is a primary basis of Qard, the rules Mubadlah should, according to some modern scholars also allow delay, to fit ithin the intention of the parties, based on analogy or "Qiyas". Intention of urse is a basic driver of the rules of contracts.

erefore, the scholars that view Mubadalah as part of the rules of Qard, have problem in the delay of the exchange when one seeks to receive change for his tes. The other scholars, who still view it as Sarf, prohibit such a delay.

owever, most scholars seem to agree that a delay is permitted if the intention as a Bai' (Sale) to begin with, as they see this as a different contract, whose tention was to purchase an item, and not exchange money for money. In a sale, erefore, the remaining change is part of the fulfillment of rights, and not part a Sarf contract, so the strict rules of Taqabud (immediate possession) do not ply.

minority does not make this difference, as for them, whenever there is a rchase, the contract splits into two separate contracts, one of Bai' (Sale), the her of Sarf (money exchange), and the rules of each apply to each part.

me scholars, who are strict on the rules of Sarf, see intention as an important ue. For them, if the intention was to do a Sarf, but the person used a Sale to de his need for Sarf, then the rules of Sarf apply, and no delay is allowed, that ould have been allowed otherwise in a Sale.

ther scholars go even further; they view the rules of Sarf applicable even in the ea of Tafadul (Inequality). Thus, for them, if the intention was Sarf to begin ith, but the lack of change necessitated that the seller offers an item in lieu of e change, then the profit on that item is illegitimate, as it breaks the rules of uality between the exchanges.

s for paper money against coins, which is common these days, some scholars gard metal coins as a different genus than paper money, and have no issues with ere being Inequality in the exchange. Other scholars do not share that view. hey see metal coins and paper money as part of the same currency, as they are

both imprinted with the state's stamp of money, and as such are the same genu
and absolute equality must be maintained.

The final remaining issue is the issue of the stipulation of a Sale, or a Servic
when a transaction of Mubadalah takes place. One scholar regards this
forbidden, although there was not much found in the literature concerning tha

I am sure that going forward, when more is written and discussed about th
very important subject, that more consensus will take place and the contract
Mubadalah or "Fakkah" will end up with a clearer set of rules.

Of course, scholars have the right to be hesitant, and to be conservative. Rib
is forbidden, in its entirety. Riba can manifest itself in many situations, wi
individuals even being completely oblivious to its presence. Especially in Sal
(Al-Buyu'), which is a favorite place to hide any intention of Riba, as th
literature attests. Which is why this subject should also be read alongside th
famous "Mudd Ajwa" concept, which is the issue of exchanging a Ribawi ite
against another Ribawi item with a non-Ribawi item included.

The trouble with that subject is that when one purchases an item, pays the mone
and receives the item and his change, it is of course somewhat of a picture
the above "Mudd Ajwa" situation, and can lead to consequences, such as the ve
interesting story from history below.

Sheikh Abdullah Bin Biyyah, Head of Al-Muwatta' Center in the UAE and
well-known scholar, recounts an interesting story of how Fuloos (Nickel an
Copper coins) were made at a particular time. He quotes Al-Maqrizi (Died Hij
845), a famous historian, who states:

> **"The reason Fuloos were made during the days of Khalifa Al-Kamil (Died Hijri 635) of the Ayyubi Dynasty was that a woman complained to Abu Taher Al-Mahalli, the Imam of the Mosque in Egypt about a situation relating to Sarf (exchange) where she had doubts. She used to buy water for half a Dirham (a Dirham is Silver) but gives a Dirham, then receives a half a Dirham, as if she bought Water and a half a Dirham for one Dirham.**

The Imam disliked this (as in the example above), and consulted the Sultan who ordered the provision of Fuloos made of other metals..." (1)

his was of course in fear of Riba as we have discussed, but there shouldn't have een worries since as we saw, such an operation is simply receiving back the nange.

arf is indeed a very difficult contract, but whatever name and rules one wishes apply to this contract, it certainly can be much more disputed than previously nought.

Iowever, what is most important is to be able to give the matter the correct iling based on its usage and not be driven easily into possible irrelevant omparisons with other contracts. This is why I end this chapter and the book ith this story from Ibn Rushd.

i his 'Bidayat Al-Mujtahid was Nihayat Al-Muqtasid", the famous Ibn Rushd Died Hijri 595) recounts an interesting allegory on Fiqh of his time, and it is iteresting that he placed it in The Book of Sarf:

"We find the (so-called) jurists of our times believing that the one who has memorized the most opinions has the greatest legal acumen. Their view is like the view of one who thought that a cobbler is he who possesses a large number of shoes and not one who has the ability to make them.

It is obvious that the person who has a large number of shoes, will, (some day), be visited by one whose feet the shoes do not fit. He will then go back to the cobbler who will make shoes that are suitable for his feet. This is the position of most of the faqihs of these times." (2)

References

(**1**) Sheikh Abdullah Bin Biyyah, "Maqasid Al-Mu'amalat wa Marasi Al-Waqi'at", (Dubai: Masar Publishing, 2018), p. 229.

(**2**) Ibn Rushd, "The Distinguished Jurist's Primer", (Reading: Garn Publishing, 1994), translated by Professor Imran Nyazee, Volume II, The Boo of Sarf, p. 233.

Glossary

AQD AL-FAKKAH: The contract of changing money into smaller denominations.

Amanah: In Trust.

Athman: What is used to pay for an item, i.e. prices.

Fadl: Increase. When two Ribawi items are exchanged unequally being of the same genus, Riba Al-Fadl occurs.

Fakk Al-Nuqud: Changing money into smaller denominations.

Fakkah: Change (as in money into smaller denominations).

Faqih: A Scholar. Plural is Fuqaha'.

Fiqh: Understanding of Shari'ah.

Fuloos: Money is small denominations made of metals other than gold or silver.

Hila: Trick or Stratagem.

Hulool: A delay in the exchange, but not very long.

Iftaa': making a fatwa.

Ijmaa': Consensus.

Illah: Operative reason for a ruling.

Irfaq: Kindness/Benevolence, a Qard is described as a contract of Irfaq.

Istifaa': Fulfillment of Rights.

Majlis: Place.

Majlis Al-Aqd: Session of Contract.

Maqasid: Purposes.

Mubadalah: Exchange based on numbers, a higher denomination note for several smaller notes.

Mudd Ajwa: A transaction in which there is an exchange of a Ribawi item against another Ribawi item with a non-Ribawi item included.

Mu'awadah: Compensatory Contract, for example a Sale contract.

Muqayadah: Exchange between two commodities (not prices).

Murabi: Person who charges Riba.

Muratalah: Exchange between the same currencies, by weight (gold for gold).

Musarafah: Sarf.

Mustafdil: A person who receives an increase in a Ribawi exchange.

Najiz: Immediate.

Al-Nasaa': Delay, mentioned in relation to Riba of Sales, as a delay between items that must be exchanged immediately.

Al-Nasee'a: Delay.

Nass: A clear legal ruling.

Niyah: Intention.

Nuqud: Plural of Naqd, meaning money.

Qabd: Possession.

Qard: Loan.

Qiyas: Analogy.

Ribawi: Specific items that have been deemed to attract Riba rules, and thus are given specific rulings for how they must be traded.

Sarf: Exchange between two different currencies (for others, it's still called Sarf even if they are the same currency).

Tafadul: Inequality in exchange.

Taqabud: Immediate Exchange between parties.

Tamathul: Equality in exchange.

Thamaniyyah: Characteristic of Value such as in money.

Wadee'a: Custody.

Wafaa': Same as Istifaa' above.

Bibliography

AAOIFI SHARI'AH STANDARDS 2017.

Al-Bahuti, "Kashaf Al-Qinaa'", (Riyadh: Dar Alam Al-Kutub, 2003).

Dr. Abbas Ahmad Al-Baz, "Ahkam Sarf Al-Nuqud wa Al-Umlat", (Amman: D
Al-Nafa'es, 1999).

Sheikh Abdulaziz bin Baz, "Fatawa Nour Ala Darb", (Riyadh: The Permane:
Committee for Scholarly Research and Ifta', 2011).

Sheikh Abdullah Bin Biyyah, "Maqasid Al-Mu'amalat wa Marasid Al-Waqi'a
(Dubai: Masar Publishing, 2018).

Al-Dardeer, "Al-Sharh Al-Sagheer", (Cairo: Dar Al-Ma'aref, 1986).

Al-Dusuqi, "Hashiat Al-Dusuqi Ala Al-Sharh Al-Kabeer", (Cairo: Dar Ihy
Al-Kutub Al-Arabiyyah).

Al-Hajjawi, "Al-Iqnaa'", (Beirut: Dar El-Marefa).

Ibn Al-Munther, "Al-Ijmaa'", (Ajman: Maktabat Al-Furqan; Ras Al-Khaima
Maktabat Makkah Al-Thaqafiah, 1999).

Ibn Al-Munther, "Al-Ishraf", (Ras Al-Khaimah: Maktabat Makkah Al-Thaqafia
2005).

Ibn Al-Qayyim, "A'alam Al-Muwaqq'in", (Al-Dammam: Dar Ibn Al-Jaw:
2002).

Ibn Qudamah, "Al-Kafi", (Giza: Dar hajr, 1997).

Ibn Qudamah, "Al-Mughni", (Riyadh: Dar Alam Al-Kutub, 1997).

Ibn Qudamah, "Al-Muqne'", (Jeddah: Maktabat Al-Sawadi, 2000), Bab Al-Ril
wa Al-Sarf, p. 169.

on Rushd (The Grandfather), "Al-Bayan wa Al-Tahsil", (Beirut: Dar Al-Gharb l-Islami, 1984).

on Rushd, "The Distinguished Jurist's Primer", (Reading: Garnet Publishing, 994), translated by Professor Imran Nyazee.

on Taymiyyah, "Al-Fatawa Al-Kubrah", (Beirut: Dar Al-Kotob Al-Ilmiyah, 987).

Majallat Al-Ahkam Al-Shar'iyyah, (Jeddah: Tihama Publications, 1981).

Al-Mawsu'a Al-Fiqhiyyah Al-Kuwaitiyyah", (Kuwait: Dar Al-Safwa Publishers, 992).

Dr. Muhammad Al-Mohaimeed, 'Ahkam Fakk Al-Nuqud", 2012.

ttp://almohaimeed.net/up/book/alnqod.pdf

l-Mu'jam Al-Waseet, (Cairo: Maktabat Al-Shurooq Al-Dawliyyah, 2004).

ahih Muslim, (Beirut: Al-Maktaba Al-Asriyyah, 2002).

heikh Muhammad bin Salih Al-Uthaimeen, "Al-Sharh Al-Mumti'", l-Dammam: Dar Ibn Al-Jawzi, 2003).

heikh Muhammad bin Salih Al-Uthaimeen, "Majmou' Fatawa", (Riyadh: Dar l-Thurayyah Publishing, 2010).

he Permanent Committee for Scholarly Research and Ifta', The Senior Council f Scholars, (Riyadh: Dar Al-Asima, 1999).

l-Qadduri, "Mukhtasar Al-Qadduri", (Beirut: Dar Al-Kotob Al-Ilmyah, 1997).

heikh Suleiman Al-Rehaily, "Dawabit Al-Riba", (Sharjah: Islamic Affairs epartment, 2015).

l-Sharbini, "Mughni Al-Muhtaj", (Beirut: Dar El-Marefa, 1997).

l-Sarakhsi, "Al-Mabsut", (Beirut: Dar El-Marefa, 1989).

Sheikh Muhammad bin Ibrahim Al-Tuwaijri, "Mawsu'at Al-Fiqh Al-Islami" (2009).

About The Author

NIZAR ALSHUBAILY is a banker with over 30 years of experience in the banking industry, having started in Islamic Banking in its early period in the 1980s.

He trained in New York, London, and Switzerland, in such institutions as Morgan Guaranty, London Business School, and IMD Lausanne. Before returning to his native Saudi Arabia. He worked in the banking industry in The City and was the head of Al-Rajhi Investment Corporation, the international investment arm of Al-Rajhi Bank, the largest Islamic bank in the world.

Nizar has held senior banking positions in several financial centers such as London, Dubai, Bahrain, and Jeddah, with some of the largest regional and international financial institutions, such as The National Commercial Bank of Saudi Arabia, and Deutsche Bank.

He writes commentaries on Islamic Banking in social media sites.

He is retired and lives in Dubai.

Don't miss out!

Visit the website below and you can sign up to receive emails whenever Nizar Abdulrahman Alshubaily publishes a new book. There's no charge and no obligation.

https://books2read.com/r/B-A-GJDX-JHRLB

BOOKS2READ

Connecting independent readers to independent writers.

Did you love *Riba In Mubadalah*? Then you should read *The Hadith Of Riba*[1] by Nizar Abdulrahman Alshubaily!

[2]

What are the main sayings of The Prophet (PEACE BE UPON HIM) on the issue of Riba?

How have they been explained by the predecessor scholars, and what rulings do they give?

Are some of the statements contradictory to the known rules of Riba?

What exceptions and disputes have arisen from the different understandings of the sayings?

In this eighth volume of Riba Revisited, the above subjects and more will be discussed and explained.

---

1. https://books2read.com/u/3JZDkv

2. https://books2read.com/u/3JZDkv